W9-AON-858

08/2019

SandCastle™

First Sounds

Wendy and Wally

Pam Scheunemann

Consulting Editor, Diane Craig, M.A./Reading Specialist

ABDO
Publishing Company

Published by ABDO Publishing Company, 4940 Viking Drive, Edina, Minnesota 55435.

Printed in the United States.

Credits
Edited by: Pam Price
Curriculum Coordinator: Nancy Tuminelly
Cover and Interior Design and Production: Mighty Media
Child Photography: Steven Wewerka, Wewerka Photography
Photo Credits: AbleStock, Brand X Pictures, Comstock, Photodisc

Library of Congress Cataloging-in-Publication Data

Scheunemann, Pam, 1955-
    Wendy and Wally / Pam Scheunemann.
        p. cm. -- (First sounds)
    Includes index.
    ISBN 1-59679-208-6 (hardcover)
    ISBN 1-59679-209-4 (paperback)
        1. English language--Consonants--Juvenile literature. I. Title. II. Series.
    PE1159.S345 2005
    428.1'3--dc22
                                                                        2004059908

SandCastle™ books are created by a professional team of educators, reading specialists, and content developers around five essential components that include phonemic awareness, phonics, vocabulary, text comprehension, and fluency. All books are written, reviewed, and leveled for guided reading, early intervention reading, and Accelerated Reader® programs and designed for use in shared, guided, and independent reading and writing activities to support a balanced approach to literacy instruction.

Let Us Know

After reading the book, SandCastle would like you to tell us your stories about reading. What is your favorite page? Was there something hard that you needed help with? Share the ups and downs of learning to read. We want to hear from you! To get posted on the ABDO Publishing Company Web site, send us e-mail at:

sandcastle@abdopub.com

SandCastle Level: Emerging

ABCDEFGH

IJKLMNOPQ

RSTUVWXYZ

abcdefgh

ijklmnopq

rstuvwxyz

Wendy

Wally

watermelon

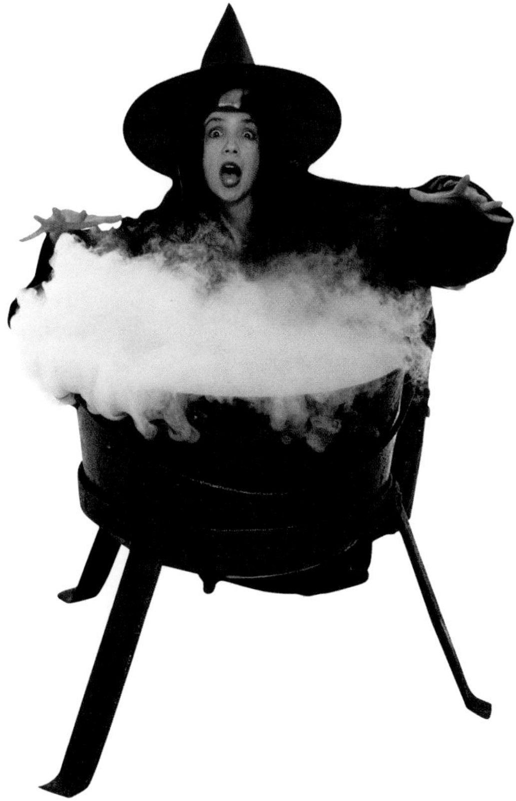

witch

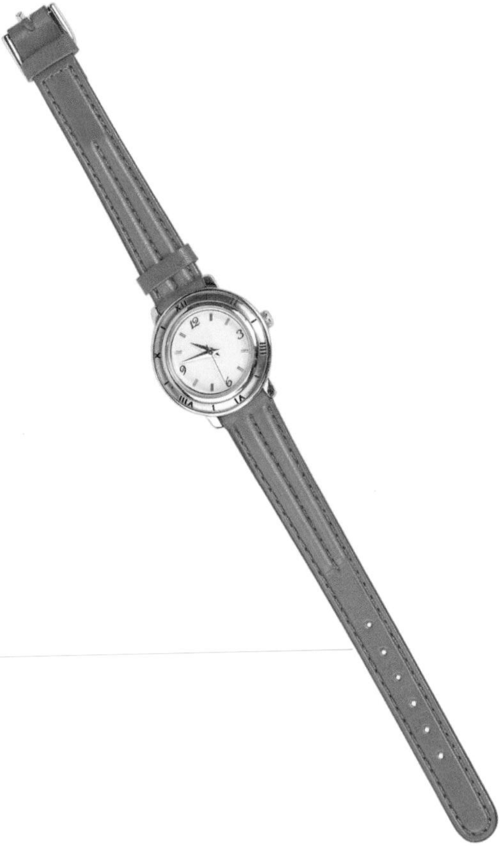

watch

window

wagon

The  is sweet.

The  is scary.

Look at the 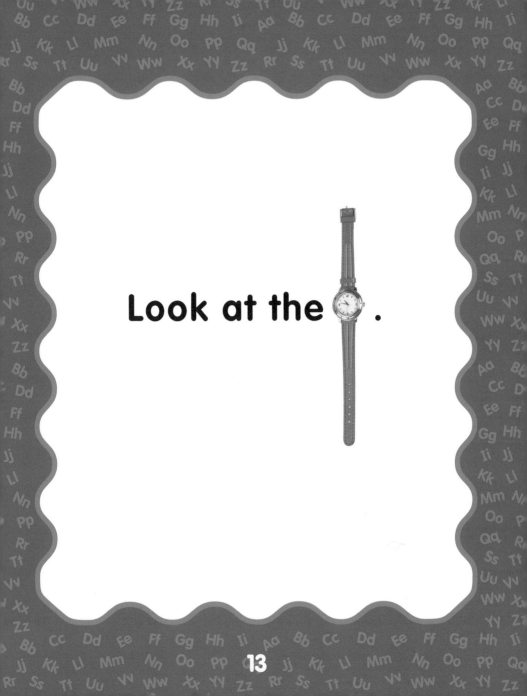 .

The  is big.

The  is red.

Wendy has a wagon.

Wally likes
watermelon.